Parables DECODED of Jesus

Study Guide

Unveiling the Mysteries of God's Kingdom through the Stories of Jesus

Volume 1: Appearances

Hany & Diana Asaad

DEDICATION

To our family, you encourage us at every step to
pursue Jesus relentlessly.

To our fellow sojourners.
May the stories Jesus told guide us all deeper into His fullness.

CONTENTS

WELCOME

Welcome to *Parables Decoded*!

Parables Decoded is a six-week journey in understanding the stories Jesus told in the context of His lifetime and applying His lessons to our lives.

Each session explores a different aspect of a parable through the lens of culture by digging deeper into the stories Jesus told. Lessons are composed of Bible study, and video and small group discussions that pulls out the richer applications. However, the real decoding happens after the video when you dive into each topic during guided small group time. Through the group discussion and the short homework, true transformation begins to unfold.

How To Use This Guide

As you'll discover, the parables of Jesus are practical. This study is designed to provide the tools so you can develop a closer spiritual walk with Jesus.

These truths will help you understand the often misinterpreted principles that have significant transforming power. Each session begins with a Bible passage, followed by explanation of the parable, and cultural relevance. The next section uncovers the reason for this parable, followed by the parable's composition, and then discussion. We wrap up each weekly study with the conclusion and homework. *Parables Decoded* moves fast, and the homework is not mandatory but highly encouraged.

The real growth in this study will happen during your small group time. There, you will process the content of the message, ask questions, and learn from others as you share what God is doing in your lives through the parables. Each session contains a bonus Middle-Eastern recipe for you to experiment and experience together if you'd like and allow the flavors of the era to cross cultures and connect us to the passages and one another.

This fill-in-the-blank guide lets you follow along together as a group while watching the videos. Answers are provided in the back.

PARABLES DECODED

Parables **DECODED** Of Jesus

Introduction to the Parables of Jesus

"But without a parable He did not speak to them." (Mark 4:34)

Stories. They define our lives. They connect us in ways that nothing else can. History and facts seem alive and relevant when sprinkled with stories. Perhaps that is why our Lord used stories to connect deep spiritual truths to everyday occurrences.

God speaks to us in many different forms in the Bible. Scripture is filled with allegories, poetry, prophecy, apocalyptic literature, and parables.

Jesus was intentional about his use of parables to convey deep spiritual truths in relevant stories that were easy for the people of the day to understand. Studying the parables is tremendously beneficial to us today, as well. Jesus made His deep messages pertinent and easy to remember. We might forget principles, but we remember stories. Parables help us apply

Biblical philosophies through easy-to-remember stories because we relate to them.

When Jesus spoke in parables, people understood the message more clearly than if He had spoken in plain truths. By digging into the customs of Jesus' day, we can have the same insights.

Let's begin to see the parables as if God were opening a small window to His Kingdom so we get to peek in. The parables provide the greatest insight to know God's heart.

Though Jesus was born in a small town and worked as a carpenter, when He spoke, it was with authority and He AMAZED everyone. Matthew 7:28-29 tells us, "[28]And so it was, when Jesus had ended these sayings, that the people were astonished at His teaching, [29]for He taught them as one having authority, and not as the scribes (NKJV)."

Jesus used ordinary people as the characters of His parables, so everyone was able to understand and relate to the story. Jesus customized His messages and used familiar things like seeds, soil and sheep to illustrate challenging truths.

For example, Jesus used a son who left his father's house and spent all his inheritance and showed the father who missed him (Luke 15:20). Jesus used a shepherd who takes care of sheep (Luke 15:4) He used a farmer who planted seeds (Matthew 13:3) and a fisherman casting nets (Matthew 13:48). Jesus spoke of a wounded man who was robbed (Luke 10:33), a widow (Luke 18:3), and a builder (Luke 14:28). He used a poor man (Luke 16:19), rich man (Luke 12:13-21), servant (Matthew 18:21-35), master (Matthew 25:14-30), and even a king (Matthew 22:1-4).

Therefore Jesus was able to touch on all aspects of life such as familial issues (Luke 15:20), agricultural life (Luke 13:6-9), investing (Matthew 25:14-30), and even politics (Luke 19:11-27) to name a few.

Parables were used by others to convey messages, but the parables of Jesus don't use imaginary, unrealistic characters like trees talking or animals speaking. Jesus is the way, the truth and life (John 14:6). His parables are good for all mankind in every generation. Jesus said in John 6:63, "The words that I speak to you are spirit, and *they* are life."

Key Elements of the Parables

1. During the ministry of Jesus, He _____ to the people in parables.

2. Jesus spoke _____ parables in the New Testament, depending on how you categorize them. For example, in Luke 5:36, we see the parables of the new and old garments and the old and new wineskins, which can be

considered one parable. But in Luke 15 Jesus uses the term "either" between the stories.

3. The parables of Jesus represent about _____ of His preaching.

4. Parables were the most _____ teachings in people's minds.

5. We can extract at least one _____ lesson from each parable.

6. Each and every parable requires a _____ from us. God might want us to start or stop something.

7. Parables can be categorized in three sections:

    a. Relationship   and   responsibilities   between _____ and you, and also _____ toward God.

    b. Relationship and responsibilities between you and your fellow _____.

    c. The believer's responsibilities toward _____- believers.

4 Questions that Frequently Arise about the Parables:

1. What does "parable" _____?

2. What are the _____?

3. Why did Christ _____ in parables?

4. How do we _____ the parables?

Q1. What does "parable" mean?

The word "parable" means:

1. The Greek word "Parabole" (Parra-Bo-lay) means to "_____ beside or _____ alongside."
2. Parable means "_____" or "_____like."
3. Parable can also mean _____.

Definition of Parable: A "parable" is an _____ story by which *a familiar idea is cast beside an unfamiliar idea* in such a way that the _____ helps people to better understand and grasp the unfamiliar idea.

Q2. What are the parables of Jesus?

Parables are:

1. Lessons taken from _____ or situations in _____.
2. Typically_____ and_____ with powerful meaning, parables teach difficult truths in a simple way.
3. Based in the context of _____ and _____.

4. _____ stories that have a _____ meaning.

5. A way of concealing _____ for believers to uncover.

6. A comparison of two things or two stories for the purpose of _____.

7. Putting something known beside something unknown to _____ the differences.

8. Relatable to _____ because they are common, ordinary stories.

Matthew13:10-13, *"¹⁰ The disciples came to him and asked, "Why do you speak to the people in parables?" ¹¹ He replied, "Because the knowledge of the __secrets__ of the kingdom of heaven has been given to you, but not to them" (NIV, emphasis added).*

Q3. Why did Christ speak in parables?

1. Because of the _____ his followers showed to hear and understand God's words.

   "Such large crowds gathered around Him that He got into a boat and sat in it, while all the people stood on the shore" (Matthew 13:2 NIV).

2. Because of the people's _____ hearts and unwillingness to _____.

> *"14 In them is fulfilled the prophecy of Isaiah: "'You will be ever hearing but never understanding; you will be ever seeing but never perceiving 15. For this people's heart has become calloused" (Matthew 13:14-15 NIV).*

3. To show us how _____ we are.

> *"For truly I tell you, many prophets and righteous people longed to see what you see but did not see it, and to hear what you hear but did not hear it" (Matthew 13:17 NIV).*

4. To _____ those who want to know the truth from everyone else.

> *"36Then Jesus sent the multitude away and went into the house. And His disciples came to Him, saying, "Explain to us the parable of the tares of the field" (Matthew13:36 NKJV).*

Parables catch us off guard and teach us about our sin in a way that will not make us defensive. The Old Testament prophet, Nathan, used a parable to convict King David of his sin. Nathan told the unsuspecting David what appeared to be a harmless story of a rich man and a poor man living in the same city (2 Samuel 12:14). The poor man owned only a single little ewe lamb he loved as a household pet while the rich man possessed large flocks; yet when the wealthy farmer had a guest to serve, he seized the poor man's single lamb for the dinner! Nathan sought to get around David's guarded exterior and cut the bonds of his self-deception to strike the moral blindness that had been veiling his vision. In a sense, Nathan's illustration was a well-laid trap because David responded with moral outrage, thus condemning himself. Nathan then applied the parable to the King's affair with Bathsheba (2 Samuel 12:5-14).

Q4. How do we interpret the parables?

You have to understand the reason Jesus chose the parable. We can interpret the parable based on the incident that caused Jesus to use the parable.

1. _____ each parable thoroughly and carefully. Look for the main truth being uncovered in the parable.
2. Do not hastily apply the _____ of one parable to another. In the parable of the sower, the seed represents the Word of God and the soil represents the human heart (Matthew 13:3-8, 18-23). However, in the

very next parable – the parable of the tares – the seed represents the children of the Kingdom and the field represents the world (Matthew 13:24-30).

3. Don't _____ anything without referring to the Bible.

4. Consider _____ and _____ events. For example, who were the Levites, Pharisees, Samaritans, etc.?

5. Learn when to stop interpreting. Don't _____. For example, Mark 12:3 states that the father believed that the tenants would respect his son, but this does not mean that the Father believed that the Jews would accept or respect His Son.

6. Preachers/Speakers might use or _____ the parable in a certain way to get their points across. Remember, the Holy Spirit can speak different messages to different people using the same parable.

7. We can _____ more than one spiritual meaning/interpretation from each parable.

8. We don't have to _____ every word mentioned in the parable. But God can shine a light on every word.

9. Do not build theological beliefs or denominational doctrines based _____ on a parable. Parables are intended to illustrate doctrine, not declare it. Do not build a whole doctrine on only one parable if

that message is not taught clearly elsewhere in the Bible. For example, teaching salvation by good works based on the parable of the sheep and goats alone would be dangerous because this doctrine is not clarified elsewhere in the Bible.

Conclusion:

❖ Don't think this Bible study is enough. Use it as a springboard to study more in depth on your own as well.

❖ Don't overlook or underestimate the parables. Parables are great treasures that help us in understanding God's mind.

❖ Comprehend the blessings and the grace of God that we were born in this day and age where the gospel, many insights, and scripture interpretations are at our disposal.

❖ The parables are copious tools for our faith walk. (Romans16:25-26)

Going forward each chapter will follow the format below:

I. **Bible Passage**

    a. **Reading**

    b. **Explanation of the Parable**

    c. **Cultural Relevance**

II. **Occasion/Reason why Jesus tells this Parable**

III. **Main Lessons (Thoughts) to Learn from the Parable**

IV. **Composition of the Parable**

V. **Discussion**

VI. **Conclusion**

VII. **Homework / Memory Verse**

VIII. **Middle-Eastern Recipe (make at home or for group study to share)**

CHAPTER 2

The Sower

Parables **⊐Ξ⊂0⊒D** of Jesus

I. Bible Passage

a. **Read Matthew 13:3-14 and Matthew 13:18-23 from NKJV**

Matthew 13:3-24, *"³ Then He spoke many things to them in parables, saying:*

"Behold, a sower went out to sow. ⁴ And as he sowed, some seed fell by the wayside; and the birds came and devoured them. ⁵ Some fell on stony places, where they did not have much earth; and they immediately sprang up because they had no depth of earth. ⁶ But when the sun was up they were scorched, and because they had no root they withered away. ⁷ And some fell among thorns, and the thorns sprang up and choked them. ⁸ But others fell on good ground and yielded a crop: some a

hundredfold, some sixty, some thirty. *9* He who has ears to hear, let him hear!"

The Purpose of Parables

"*10* And the disciples came and said to Him, 'Why do You speak to them in parables?'

11 He answered and said to them, "Because it has been given to you to know the mysteries of the kingdom of heaven, but to them it has not been given. *12* For whoever has, to him more will be given, and he will have abundance; but whoever does not have, even what he has will be taken away from him. *13* Therefore I speak to them in parables, because seeing they do not see, and hearing they do not hear, nor do they understand. *14* And in them the prophecy of Isaiah is fulfilled, which says: 'Hearing you will hear and shall not understand, And seeing you will see and not perceive; *15* For the hearts of this people have grown dull. Their ears are hard of hearing, And their eyes they have closed, Lest they should see with their eyes and hear with their ears, Lest they should understand with their hearts and turn, So that I should heal them.'*16* But blessed are your eyes for they see, and your ears for they hear; *17* for assuredly, I say to you that many prophets and righteous men desired to see what you see, and did not see it, and to hear what you hear, and did not hear it.

The Parable of the Sower Explained

18 "Therefore hear the parable of the sower: *19* When anyone hears the word of the kingdom, and does not understand it, then the wicked one comes and snatches away what was sown in his *heart. This is he who received seed by the wayside. [20] But he who received the seed on stony places, this is he who hears the word and immediately receives it with joy; [21] yet he has no root in himself, but endures only for a while. For when tribulation or persecution arises because of the word, immediately he stumbles. [22] Now he who received seed among the thorns is he who hears the word, and the cares of this world and the deceitfulness of riches choke the word, and he becomes unfruitful. [23] But he who received seed on the good ground is he who hears the word and understands it, who indeed bears fruit and produces: some a hundredfold, some sixty, some thirty."*

b. Explanation of the Parable

A farmer went out to plant seeds. Some of the seeds fell on the wayside (where people walk). But these seeds were easy for birds to spot, and the birds came and devoured them. Other seeds fell on stony places. The seeds sprouted a little, but because there wasn't deep earth, they were scorched when the sun came out. More seeds fell on thorny ground. These seeds had a chance to grow, but the thorns choked them and killed them. Last, some seeds fell on good ground and these seeds were able to bear fruit.

This parable was chronicled _____ times in the New Testament: Matthew 13:3-23, Mark 4:2-20, and Luke 8:4-15. This parable talks about the outcome of _____ that fell on different types of _____.

c. Cultural Relevance

Jesus was speaking to an audience that understood agriculture. They were familiar with seeds and the type of ground needed to cultivate good fruit. They would have been familiar with how precious the seeds were, and in talking about how the seeds were haphazardly strewn about, Jesus painted a picture of a farmer with a generous, open grip on his seeds. This concept may have been challenging to an audience familiar with farming.

1. When was this message preached?
    a. It was expounded upon after Jesus had _____ preached this same message to other people previously in the day.

2. To whom was it preached?
    a. The great _____ (at least 5,000 people) and everyone who has ears to hear.

3. Where was it preached and why?
    a. The _____.
    b. Although a _____ theater would have been more fitting for a King, Jesus made the best of His surroundings. Humble enough to use nature, and taking advantage of his surroundings, Jesus set the example, inviting and accessible to all, not exclusive.
    c. His pulpit was a _____ – Jesus used what was available to Him.

4. What is a seed?

    a. Seeds are the first form of life. Although they seem

      _____ and _____ on

      their own, seeds contain all the potential to become

      an orchard.

If you want to share the gospel with someone, what "platform" could you use?

_____

_____

_____

_____

_____

_____

In your own words, what seeds do you have that can be shared or planted in someone else's life?

_____

_____

_____

_____

_____

_____

II. Occasion/Reason why Jesus tells this parable

People gathered around Jesus to hear Him. *"And great multitudes were gathered together unto him, so that he went into a ship, and sat; and the whole multitude stood on the shore" (Matthew 13:2 NKJV).*

NOTES:_____

_____

_____

_____

III. Main lessons (thoughts) from the parable

a. To prepare our _____ before listening to God's Word

b. To understand how the _____ steals God's word from our lives

c. To _____ us how to interpret parables. This parable is the key to understanding all parables. Mark 4:13 states it this way. "Then Jesus said to them, "Don't you understand this parable? How then will you understand any parable?" (NIV).

d. To teach that God _____ looks for fruit and harvest

NOTES:_____

_____

IV. Composition of the sower parable

The Sower Parable is made up of three important elements:

The _____ - the _____ - and the

_____

1. The **sower** represents _____, who came from _____ to plant His Word. The sower can also represent ministers spreading God's word.

2. The **seeds** represent the _____ of God.

3. The **soil** represents _____ (or people's minds)

NOTES:_____

_____

_____

_____

_____

_____

_____

_____

_____

_____

_____

_____

_____

V.   Discussion:

➢ One kind of seed (or word of God) exists. But Jesus reveals four kinds of hearts where the seeds fall.

1. Wayside (hard ground):

Represents those who _____ God's Word but don't pay attention. The Word of God goes in one ear and out the other. Their _____ and _____ are closed, leaving no room for God's Word in their lives. These individuals are easy prey for Satan. The Devil snatches the Word **before** it can spring up. These people are usually mindless, careless hearers.

   a. The wayside represents someone who hears, but the Word doesn't move him or her at all. In the wayside soil, the enemy is _____.

    b. How to fix the wayside (hard) ground:

        i. Break up the ground by preparing our hearts for the Word and humbling ourselves.

        ii. Cover the seed. "Your word I have hidden in my heart, that I might not sin against You" (Psalm 119:11 NIV).

Can you recall a time where your mind or heart was the wayside?

_____

_____

_____

_____

_____

_____

Have you corrected the wayside mindset? How?

_____

_____

_____

_____

_____

_____

2. Stony places (shallow ground):

Those who get _____ -up when they hear God's Word but quickly go back to old ways. This happens when people lack _____ in the Word. The Enemy is the _____.

    a. A good farmer would remove any rocks from the land. The stony way is a thin layer of dirt with rocks underneath. The seed could spring up quickly, but all the growth will be upward and not down because the ground has no depth. An inexperienced farmer would be happy for the fast growth. But the plant dries and dies fast when the sun comes out because it has no roots. Stony places represent a person's emotions. Jesus described someone who reacts to the Word of God when they hear it but soon forgets it. King Herod was similar to that. He admired John the Baptist, but when John confronted him about marrying Herodia, Herod didn't repent (remove the rocks). Instead, he had John the Baptist killed.

b. How to fix the stony ground heart: grace, truth, and accountability.

Can you recall a time where your mind or heart was the stony/shallow ground?

_____

_____

_____

_____

_____

_____

Have you corrected the shallow ground mindset? How?

_____

_____

_____

_____

_____

_____

3. **Thorns (distracted hearts)**:

This third person described is too _____ with life. These people face problems in life that cause them to _____ God or get _____ at God.

   a. This type of soil has become "unfruitful", which means they were fruitful at some point.

   b. The thorny way represents a divided heart. This heart has so many cares that divert them from God. David said in Psalm 86, "Unite my heart."

   c. What's your distraction?

Thorns choke in 3 areas:

       1. Cares of this world

       2. The deceitfulness of riches

       3. Desiring the world

   d. The enemy is the _____.

   e. How to fix the thorny ground: Give it to God.

Can you recall a time where your mind was thorny ground?

_____

_____

_____

_____

_____

_____

_____

Have you corrected the thorny ground mindset? How?

_____

_____

_____

_____

_____

_____

_____

4. Good Ground:

Those who hear the Word and _____ it. They are fruitful. How close you are to the Water (Holy Spirit) determines how fruitful you are. Some bear fruit and produce: some a hundredfold, some sixty, some thirty. Naturally, as humans we do not have good ground. That's why in Jeremiah 4 we are instructed, "don't plant in thorns. "If you want to have good ground, dig up your heart and pick out the rocks by repenting. Then when the seed falls in your heart, it falls on good ground. Good ground needs preparation.

As Christians, our goal is to cultivate good ground. How can you become and remain good ground?

_____

_____

At first glance, all four grounds appear similar. What are the differentiating factors between each ground?

_____

_____

VI. Conclusion

In this parable Jesus warns us to avoid the unclean trinity.

Unclean Trinity

We believe the Holy Trinity is God the Father, God the Son, and God the Holy Spirit as one.

"For there are three that bear witness in heaven: the Father, the Word, and the Holy Spirit; and these three are one" (1 John 5:7 NKJV).

God appears to us as three persons, each with His own identity and job in our lives yet all three are one. The enemy considers himself to be "like God" with his own trinity – the "unholy trinity". We know that the battle is won and our Lord is victorious, but that doesn't stop the enemy from fighting us.

The unholy trinity is the _____, the _____, and the _____. And Jesus alludes to all three in this parable. Through the Bible, we see this concept repeated. Usually, the world fights the Father, the devil fights Jesus, and the flesh fights the Holy Spirit.

We see the Holy Trinity together during the baptism of Jesus in Matthew 3. As Jesus was baptized, the Holy Spirit appeared as a dove and we hear the voice from Heaven saying, "This is my beloved son". We also see the unholy trinity together during the temptation of Jesus in the very next chapter, Matthew 4. The devil first asked Jesus to turn the rock into bread (flesh is fighting). Then, the devil asked Jesus to throw Himself of the temple (the Devil is fighting). And finally the devil asked Jesus to bow down and worship him with the promise of giving Jesus the world (the world is fighting). (This concept is expanded in the companion book *Parables Decoded: Volume 1*).

VII.   Homework:

For Reflection:

We must look at our fruit.
- o   What are we producing?
- o   What is the quality of my fruit? The quality of the fruit is subject to the quality of the soil (our hearts).
- o   Where am I not producing or holding back?
- o   What are the results of the life I am living?
- o   In what areas has the enemy been fighting me?

_____

_____

_____

_____

_____

- -   Remember where the Parable of the Sower is mentioned – Matthew 13:3-23, Mark 4:2-20, and Luke 8:4-15.

- What new insights have you gleaned from the Parable of the Sower presented from this perspective?

_____

_____

_____

_____

_____

_____

_____

_____

_____

_____

_____

_____

_____

_____

_____

_____

_____

_____

_____

_____

_____

VIII.   Middle-Eastern Recipe

FITEER MESHALTET
Egyptian Layered Pastry

This dish is essentially a layered pastry that can be eaten with a wide variety of toppings, ranging from sweet ishta (cream) to salty feta cheese, honey or a mix of molasses and tahini. The following recipe is a simplified version of fiteer meshaltet, but the more times the layers are repeated, the better the outcome.

INGREDIENTS:

2 cups Flour

½ cup Water

½ tsp Salt

¼ tsp Sugar

½ cup Clarified or Melted Butter

Vegetable oil, for greasing

METHOD

Sift the flour then make a well in the middle and add in water, salt, and sugar. Mix the dough well to a smooth consistency, then knead and stretch dough several times for about 10 minutes.

Shape the dough into a smooth ball. Flatten slightly and place on a large baking sheet liberally greased with vegetable oil. Cover loosely with cling film and leave the dough to rest for about 30 minutes. Using a rolling pin, spread the dough ball paper thin, pushing out at the edges all around gently, so as not to tear the dough. Generously brush the dough with melted clarified butter then fold over from all sides and repeat about 6 times (coating each time with the melted butter). Shape the dough into a circle about 12 inches in diameter. Place the dough on a butter greased baking sheet then bake at 350 degrees for 20-30 minutes until golden brown.

Fiteer meshaltet can be served sweet topped with cream, honey and crushed nuts or savory, topped with feta cheese.

CHAPTER 3

The Ten Virgins

Parables ===== **DECODED** ===== Of Jesus

I. Bible Passage

a. Reading Matthew 25:1-13 NIV

"*[1] At that time the kingdom of heaven will be like ten virgins who took their lamps and went out to meet the bridegroom. [2] Five of them were foolish and five were wise. [3] The foolish ones took their lamps but did not take any oil with them. [4] The wise ones, however, took oil in jars along with their lamps. [5] The bridegroom was a long time in coming, and they all became drowsy and fell asleep. " [6]At midnight the cry rang out: 'Here's the bridegroom! Come out to meet him!' "[7]Then all the virgins woke up and trimmed their lamps. [8]The foolish ones said to the wise, 'Give us some of your oil; our lamps are going out.' " [9]No,' they replied, 'there may not be enough for both us and you. Instead, go to those who sell oil and buy some for yourselves.' "[10]But while they were on their way to buy the oil, the bridegroom arrived. The virgins who were ready went in with him to the wedding banquet. And the door was shut. . "[11]Later the others also came. 'Lord, Lord,' they said, 'open the door for us!'*

"[12]But he replied, 'Truly I tell you, I don't know you.' "[13]Therefore keep watch, because you do not know the day or the hour."

b.   Explanation of the parable

The parable of the ten virgins opens a small window into the Kingdom of Heaven. The Kingdom of Heaven is likened to ten virgins (similar to bridesmaids) who were invited to a wedding. All ten girls had lit oil lamps. Five planned ahead and took extra oil for when the oil ran out. Jesus describes these girls as "wise". The other five filled their lamps with oil but didn't carry/take spare oil. Jesus describes these girls as "foolish". The groom was late and all the girls fell asleep. At midnight, they awoke to people shouting, "The groom is coming – the groom is coming". When the lamps ran out of oil, the five wise girls simply added their spare oil. The five foolish girls needed more oil. So they asked the wise girls to share. The wise girls said no because they did not have enough to share The wise girls suggested that the foolish girls go buy more oil. While they were away, the groom arrived. He took those who were ready into the house and started the wedding ceremony. The foolish girls came back too late. They knocked on the door and asked the groom to let them in, but the groom replied He didn't know them. Jesus then said to those gathered, "The truth

is, you will never know when I'll come back…so be ready."

c. Cultural Relevance

Two stages comprised a Jewish marriage: Ketubbeh (engagement) and ceremony.

1. The **Ketubbeh** (betrothal stage) was a _____ agreement.

   a. The Ketubbah was a _____ binding document. The primary purpose was to protect the bride, though she did not even sign it. The father of the bride used his wisdom to look out for his daughter's best interests.

   b. Ketubbeh is the _____ stage of a Jewish marriage but we incorporate it into the latter stages of modern weddings with the signing of the legal marriage license.

   c. "Courting" (get-to-know-you stage) began _____ the couple were "espoused" in the Ketubbeh.

   d. After the Ketubbah was signed, only a legal _____ could dissolve the betrothal.

   e. The bride remained completely under her father's _____ and lived with him.

f. The groom and the father of the bride _____ a legal document with clear terms.

g. _____ money was to be paid to the father by the groom.

"Ask me ever so much dowry and gift, and I will give according to what you say to me; but give me the young woman as a wife" (Genesis 34:12 NKJV).

h. The betrothed couple was not allowed to _____ together during their betrothal, but they were considered "legally married".

*"If a man happens to meet in a town a **virgin** pledged to be married and he sleeps with her, you shall take both of them to the gate of that town and stone them to death—the young woman because she was in a town and did not scream for help, and the man because he violated **another man's wife**. You must purge the evil from among you" (Deuteronomy 22:21-23 NIV emphasis added).*

i. Unfaithfulness during betrothal was considered _____.

Notes:

_____

_____

2. The Jewish marriage reached the second stage at the _____, which began with the groom taking the bride from her father's house. This is also considered a bridal festival.

    a. When the groom had fulfilled the financial and legal _____ of the Ketubah to the satisfaction of the bride's father, the elder would set a date for the ceremony.

    b. The bride and the groom might have up to _____ friends witness the event.

    c. The bride left her father's _____ with her groom to begin the bridal festival.

    d. The bride and groom walked all over the town to receive congratulations and gifts from as many people as possible. Then they entered their own home, and the festivities continued for a week. During the week, the bride and groom were treated like _____.

Jacob worked seven years to marry Rachel, after being tricked and marrying Leah, he waited a week to marry Rachel, but he had to work another seven years for Rachel (see Genesis 29:18-30).

Notes:_____

_____

_____

II. Occasion/Reason why Jesus tells this Parable

Jesus answered the disciples' question in Matthew 24:3, "As Jesus was sitting on the Mount of Olives, the disciples came to him privately. "Tell us," they said, "when will this happen, and what will be the sign of your coming and of the end of the age?" (NIV).

III. Main Lesson of this Parable

a. That we are to be _____ and _____ (from the inside) for the second coming of Jesus Christ.

b. Salvation cannot be _____ down or given by man.

c. Each person is responsible for his/her own salvation by _____ Jesus as Lord and Savior.

d. This parable clarifies the major differences between _____ and _____.

e. Old Testament salvation is not the _____ as New Testament salvation.

IV. Composition of the Parable

a. The ten virgins represent those who are _____ to attend the feast, which is salvation through the death and resurrection of Jesus.

b. Lit lamps represent the _____ of God.

   "Your word is a lamp for my feet, a light on my path" (Psalm 119:105 NIV).

c. Oil represents the _____ Spirit.

   "So Samuel took the horn of oil and anointed him in the presence of his brothers, and from that day on the Spirit of the Lord came powerfully upon David" (1 Samuel16:13 NIV).

d. Insufficient oil represents a _____ of spiritual preparation.

e. Enough oil represents the _____ with the Holy Spirit.

f. Purchasing oil represents trying (with our own effort) to get our spiritual lives in _____.

g. The bridegroom represents Jesus _____.

h. The ceremony represents the _____ of the Lamb.

i. The closed door represents that once the Feast of the Lamb _____, no one can enter.

Notes:_____

_____

_____

V. Discussion

1.   In Matthew 24:3, Jesus answered the question about the signs of His second coming with two parables that conclude no one knows the time or the _____, and we need to be ready at all times. The first parable, "The Ten Virgins", focuses on being saved and ready for His second coming. This should be an assurance of what we have on the inside because no one can see with natural eyes wisdom or foolishness. The second parable, "The Talents", focuses on being saved and ready for His second coming. Our faith should show on the outside as we minister to others.

2.   **In this parable, all ten virgins are alike on the _____. Consider these commonalities. All :**

O Heard the Calling   O Were invited to Participate

O Brought their Own Lamps   O Had Lamps Filled with Oil

O Fell Asleep   O Waited for the Groom to Come

3.   They might look the _____ from the outside, but they are not the _____ from the inside! Five were wise, and five were foolish. In addition, because we, as humans, cannot see the inside, Jesus wants us to

be aware of what's inside. We might look wise on the outside, but we could be foolish. We could be rich on the outside but poor inside. We could be healthy on the outside but wounded. Good looking on the outside but ugly inside. The list can go on and on. In other words, we might not see the difference externally, but we surely can see the results of inside motivation.

4. Also note: Ten represents the _____ and five represents _____ in Bible number representations.

5. The ten virgins can also represent the whole _____. The five wise virgins represent the true _____ of Christ.

6. Today's church is varied, for the most part. Many say they are "Christian," but that title is merely a _____, not a real relationship. Within the vast array of the "church" itself is the true body of Christ.

7. The oil in scripture represents the Holy Spirit. Some try to do the work of the ministry and the work of the gospel in their _____ and the abilities of their flesh only. But others walk in the Spirit and are filled with the Spirit. They trust the Spirit to guide and build the church. Paul tells us in

Romans 8:14, "But as many as are led by the Spirit of God, they are the sons of God".

8. So those foolish virgins who had their lamps, but no oil were significant. Notice they all were lumped into one party until that final cry, and then their real _____ was exposed. The foolish virgins lacking the oil began to trim the wicks and said, "Oh, our lamps are going out." They realized only then that they didn't have the true light, but it was too late. While they were gone to buy oil, the bridegroom came. Those who were ready went into the marriage feast of the lamb. Those who were foolish came back and said, "Open to us," but the Lord said, "I don't know you."

9. Therefore, be ready. Not only that, but follow the command given to us throughout the New Testament: Walk in the Spirit. Be led by the Spirit. Depend upon the Spirit of God. Be filled with the Spirit. And watch, therefore, because you don't know when the Lord is _____.

Notes:

_____

_____

_____

_____

Explanation of the "Foolish"

The Word of God clearly describes the foolish throughout the Old and New testaments. Here are some descriptions:

1. *Foolish* is the one who _____ God's existence.

   "The fool says in his heart, 'There is no God'" (Psalm 14:1 NIV).

2. Foolish is the one who _____ on him/herself.

   "Those who trust in themselves are fools, but those who walk in wisdom are kept safe" (Proverbs 28:26 NIV).

3. Foolish is one who listens to God's words and _____ live   it.

   "But everyone who hears these words of mine and does not put them into practice is like a foolish man who built his house on sand"(Matt 7:26 NIV).

4. A foolish person is the one who _____ God.

   "His wife said to him, "Are you still maintaining your integrity? Curse God and die!" He replied, "You are talking like a foolish woman. Shall we accept good from God, and not trouble?" In all this, Job did not sin in what he said" (Job 2:9-10 NIV).

5. A foolish person is one who doesn't differentiate between _____ and darkness.

"The wise have eyes in their heads, while the fool walks in the darkness" (Ecclesiastes 2:14 NIV).

6. Foolish is the one who has a _____ temper.

"A quick-tempered person does foolish things" (Proverbs 14:17 NIV).

7. The foolish man is the one who has _____ speech.

"Better the poor whose walk is blameless than a fool whose lips are perverse" (Proverbs 19:1 NIV).

8. The foolish person doesn't believe in the message of the _____.

"For the message of the cross is foolishness to those who are perishing, but to us who are being saved it is the power of God" (1 Corinthians 1:18 NIV).

Important Key:

The Bible never describes believers as fools.

Notes:

_____

_____

_____

_____

_____

Explanation of the "Wise"

A wise person is the _____ of the foolish person. The wise believe that God exists, rely on God, live the word, honor God, know Jesus is the light of the world, exercise patience, think before speaking, and believe in the message of the cross.

Nevertheless, we would like to add extra benefits of being a wise person.

1. **God will _____ you up and put you in charge**.

   "The Lord answered, "Who then is the faithful and wise manager, whom the master puts in charge of his servants to give them their food allowance at the proper time?" (Matthew 12:42 NIV).

2. **You are wise for your own _____**.

   "If you are wise, your wisdom will reward you; if you are a mocker, you alone will suffer" (Proverbs 9:12 NIV).

Notes:

_____

_____

_____

_____

Explanation of the "Bridegroom"

The bridegroom is Jesus, who died on the cross to
_____ the price (dowry) to bring us as a pure virgin
to Himself, set apart, _____ to no one but Him.

Explanation of the "Oil"

The oil signifies the Holy Spirit and in this parable is a
_____ of our Salvation.

The Parable of the Ten Virgins requires an understanding that salvation through Christ alone is the only way. Appearing saved or trying to earn deliverance (or buy it like the foolish virgins) will never suffice. When the day comes, neither family, friends, nor anyone else can save your soul. Salvation cannot be borrowed or handed down from parents. God has only "children" not "grandchildren". We can learn from others, understand the Bible through others, and we can even be led to Christ through others, but only Jesus can provide salvation.

"Do not put your trust in princes, in human beings, who cannot save"(Psalm 146:3 NIV).

Without salvation and the Holy Spirit, our lives would be empty and we would live in total darkness. Many people try to purchase redemption. Can God be bought or bribed? No! Salvation is precious and nothing we own or could do can pay for it. We simply cannot afford it, and we cannot afford to live without it.

Life Application

- Are you a wise person who has accepted Jesus as Lord and Savior or are you pretending to be wise? What does salvation mean to you?

_____

_____

_____

_____

_____

- Have you been anointed by the oil of the Holy Spirit? How can you seek God for this?

_____

_____

_____

_____

_____

- We pray that you would be wise enough either to have made this choice or make it right now. What does that decision look like in your life?

_____

_____

_____

_____

_____

VI.   Conclusion

Today, our churches are full of true Christians (wise) and others who appear to be Christians. The Bible describes it in 2 Timothy 3:5 as having a form of godliness but denying its power. Consider real and plastic flowers. From afar, they look alike. But as you get closer, the flowers are completely different. The fake flowers have no smell, which is a sign of no life. Once you examine fake believers, you can tell the difference, as well.

We must accept the Lord today and not delay. The door will close. In the Old Testament, Noah preached salvation to the people and no one listened. Every time Noah hammered in a nail, he sent a message for all to come into the ark before the door closed. Suddenly, the door closed and it didn't matter who was standing outside the ark door or who was 1,000 miles away. Everyone outside perished.

Jesus is the ark and the door, would you come in?

VII. Homework

Examine yourself under the leadership of the Holy Spirit. Are you one of the wise or one of the fools? Are you sure you are 100% ready for Jesus to come again? If not, this is a perfect opportunity to make that decision.

Dear Lord, thank you that you are patient with me and Your desire is that none perish. Thank you for sending your son, Jesus, to die in my place. I accept His willing sacrifice and receive your forgiveness of all my sins. Lead my life and guide me in your paths, I pray. In Jesus' name, Amen.

Notes:

_____

_____

_____

               _____

               _____

               _____

               _____

VIII.   Middle-Eastern Recipe

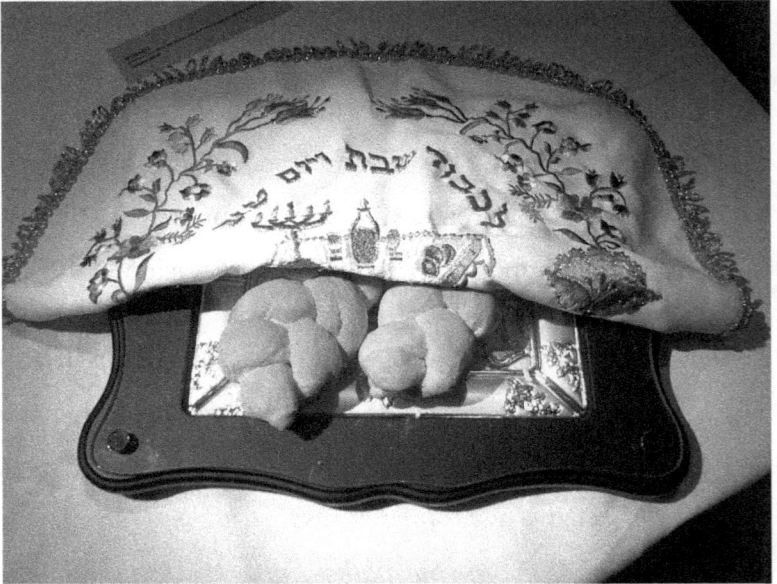

DIANA'S CHALLAH BREAD

(makes 2 loaves)

INGREDIENTS

6 cups white flour

1/2 c oil

1/4 c sugar

1 1/2 T yeast

2 cups water warm

2 eggs (room temp)

2 T Kosher salt

Sesame seeds if desired

Egg wash:

    1 egg

    ¼ tsp vanilla

    1 tsp sugar

For serving:

    Olive oil

    Kosher salt

    Olives

    Cheese

METHOD

Add water and yeast (sprinkled on top) to a stand mixer with the paddle attachment. Let sit for 10 minutes. Heat oven to 200 degrees then turn it off . (Dough will rise in the cooling oven.)

Slowly mix small amounts of flour on medium while adding other ingredients as directed. Add sugar and salt. Add another scoop of flour slowly. Then add eggs and finish by gradually adding remaining flour. Add oil. Dough will be sticky. Cover bowl loosely with plastic wrap and place in the oven you turned off at the beginning for one hour to double in size. Oil counter and divide risen dough in half then split each half into three portions. Roll each ball into long logs out. Keep rolling the dough to extend the length to about 20 inches. Connect three strands at top and braid the bread middle strand over the top. Place bread on lightly oiled baking sheet.

To make egg wash, mix one egg, a splash of vanilla, and 1 teaspoon of sugar. Brush over braided dough. Add sesame seeds if you like. Preheat oven to 400 degrees. Let dough rest for 10 minutes before baking on a low rack for 12 to 17 minutes.

Break the bread and dip in olive oil and kosher salt. Serve with olives and cheese. Enjoy.

CHAPTER 4

The Wedding Feast

Parables

d≡C0)≡D

Of Jesus

I. Bible Passage

a. Reading from the Bible: Matthew 22:1-13 NKJV

"[1]And Jesus answered and spoke to them again by parables and said: [2] "The kingdom of heaven is like a certain king who arranged a marriage for his son, [3] and sent out his servants to call those who were invited to the wedding; and they were not willing to come. [4]Again, he sent out other servants, saying, 'Tell those who are invited, "See, I have prepared my dinner; my oxen and fatted cattle are killed, and all things are ready. Come to the wedding."' [5] But

they made light of it and went their ways, one to his own farm, another to his business. [6] And the rest seized his servants, treated them spitefully, and killed them. [7] But when the king heard about it, he was furious. And he sent out his armies, destroyed those murderers, and burned up their city. [8] Then he said to his servants, 'The wedding is ready, but those who were invited were not worthy. [9] Therefore go into the highways, and as many as you find, invite to the wedding.' [10] So those servants went out into the highways and gathered together all whom they found, both bad and good. And the wedding hall was filled with guests.

[11] *"But when the king came in to see the guests, he saw a man there who did not have on a wedding garment. [12] So he said to him, 'Friend, how did you come in here without a wedding garment?' And he was speechless. [13] Then the king said to the servants, 'Bind him hand and foot, take him away, and cast him into outer darkness; there will be weeping and gnashing of teeth.' [14] "For many are called, but few are chosen."*

b. Explanation of the Parable

A certain king was arranging a wedding ceremony for his son.. When he sent his servants to call the invited guests to the wedding, they were not willing to attend. The king sent more servants to those who were invited to tell the guests "to see" dinner is ready. Just come to the wedding. But they did not care. . One of the invitees went to his farm, another went to his business, and the rest mistreated and killed the king's servants. The king was furious when he heard what happened. So he sent his armies to destroy the murderers and burn their city.

The king said to his remaining servants, the wedding is ready, but those who are invited are not worthy of attending. Therefore go into the highways and the streets and invite as many as you find. The servants did exactly what the king asked of them and gathered people, both bad and good. The wedding hall was filled with guests. One of the guests was not wearing a wedding garment, so the king asked him, "Friend, how did you come in here without a wedding garment?" He was speechless. Then the king said to his servants, bind his hands and feet, take him away, and cast him into the outer darkness, there will be weeping and gnashing of teeth. Then Jesus makes a statement that many of us don't understand: For many are called, but few are chosen.

c. Cultural Relevance

Weddings are joyful events. In fact, in the Middle East, people use the word JOY instead of "wedding". For example, someone going to a wedding would say, "We are going to joy". Everyone who was invited customarily attended. Not attending would offend the parents of the groom and bride, especially the groom's father. After a wedding date was set, the father sent a formal invitation to all guests of honor. On the day of the marriage ceremony, servants would go to let the invitees know that dinner is served. Nevertheless, rejecting a king's invitation was insulting and considered treason or a declaration of war.

II. Occasion/Reason why Jesus Tells this Parable

Jesus was answering a question from the Pharisees. *"By what authority are You doing these things? And who gave You this authority?" (Matthew 21:23 NKJV)*. The Parable of the Wedding Feast was Jesus' answer to their question.

III. Main Lesson of the Parable

a. God has invited us, but our _____ will determine our destiny.

b. Salvation is through _____ and is not based on our own worthiness.

c. God prepared everything for us, and all we need to do is _____ the invitation to attend and enjoy what He has done for us.

d. God's _____ is extended to everyone, bad and good.

e. Stop using _____ for not believing that Jesus is Lord.

f. A time will come when God _____ His invitation.

g. God repeatedly _____ invitations. (Do not delay.)

h. God is _____ and patient.

IV. **Composition of the Parable**

King = God the Father

Son = God the Son

Wedding = Supper of the covenant or supper of the lamb

Invitation = God offers the option to be part if His kingdom

Oxen Killed = Sacrifice has been offered

Servants = Prophets, as well as men and women of God (in this parable, could possibly mean John the Baptist)

Armies = Angels

Invitees = Nation of Israel

Everyone else = all other nations

Farm = Cares of the flesh

Business = Loving the world

Highways = Anyone passing through the city, including beggars or the homeless

Wedding garment = Salvation

Outer darkness = Hell

V. Discussion

a. Things to keep in mind:

  i. The first invitation was not actually the first invitation. The first invitation was sent when the marriage was announced.

  ii. Jews had no excuses because they had advance notice that the Messiah was coming. And the Pharisees had seen John the Baptist "showing" them that dinner was served. (The Messiah is here.)

  iii. The king showed his patience a second time in the parable by extending the invitation by sending the servants again to let the guests know that dinner was ready. The king even wanted to whet their appetites and let them know the oxen and fatted cattle had been prepared.

  iv. The honored guests refused to attend the wedding because they were preoccupied with worldly things and not eternal life. Jesus wanted to point out again that we should not be preoccupied with temporal things.

The Gospels contain a few "Trio-Parables". For example, the parable of the lost sheep, lost coin, and lost son in Luke 15 represent the Father, the Son, and the Holy Spirit. The Marriage Feast parable is also a "Trio-Parable". The parable of the father and two sons, the parable of the rejected son, and this parable of the Marriage Feast, also can represent the Father, the Son, and the work of the Holy Spirit.

These "Trio-Parables" show two sides. One side shows that man was unable to please God by trying to keep the law on his own. The other side shows God's grace that works in people who are undeserving.

b) Quick Review to Better Understand the Parable

Question: What is the Kingdom of Heaven?

The Kingdom of Heaven is not the same as Heaven. The Kingdom of Heaven is not a kingdom **in** Heaven. The Kingdom of Heaven is on the earth and it's comprised of those who proclaim that Jesus is Lord. For example, Jesus said the kingdom of Heaven is like ten virgins, five wise and five foolish. Heaven doesn't have anyone foolish or evil.

Jesus usually answered questions with another question, especially to those who were crooked or ignored the truth. In the Marriage Feast parable, Jesus answered the question, *"By what authority are You doing these things? And who gave You this authority?" (Matthew 21:23 NKJV)* by asking a question about John the Baptist. Was the baptism of John from Heaven or man? The Pharisees felt as though this was a trick question. If they said it was from Heaven, then Jesus might ask why they didn't get baptized. And the people would be angry if the Pharisees answered that the baptism of John was from man, as they believed John was a prophet of God. So the Pharisees replied, "We don't know." What Jesus was saying is, *if you knew the answer to my question, you would know the answer to your own question.*

Jesus decided to answer His question to the Pharisees first with the parable of the two sons. Then He answered their question with a second parable, the parable of the rejected son. As we will see, Jesus was not trying to escape answering their question, because He answered it clearly. And finally He used the third parable to make an important point about grace.

The first parable that was a direct reply to their question was about a father having two sons. He asked the first son to go work in his field and the son said no, but then, the son felt bad and went to work. Then the father asked his second son to go work in the field. The second son said he would go, but he never actually went to the field. Jesus then asked which son did the will of the Father. The Pharisees answered the first son. Jesus said to them, *"Assuredly, I say to you that tax collectors and harlots enter the kingdom of God before you. 32 For John came to you in the way of righteousness, and you did not believe him; but tax collectors and harlots believed him; and when you saw it, you did not afterward relent and believe him" (Matthew 21:31-32 NKJV).* Jesus was saying that the tax collectors and harlots who initially said no to God's call and later accepted were better off than those who answered, "Yes" and did nothing.

The second parable revealed a landowner who planted a

vineyard and leased it to vinedressers and then traveled away. When harvest time came, the landowner sent his servants to collect the fruit. The vinedresser beat, killed, and stoned the servants. The landowner sent more servants, and the vinedresser did likewise to them. Finally, the landowner sent his son, thinking, "They will respect my son." But they also killed the son thinking they could take over his inheritance.

Jesus asked them, "When the owner of the vineyard comes, what will he do to those vinedressers?" They answered, "He will destroy those wicked men miserably, and lease *his* vineyard to other vinedressers who will render to him the fruits in their seasons." And because the Pharisees were religious leaders, they knew that the vineyard represented the nation of Israel and the owner was God. The servants were the prophets. Notice that Jesus never called the religious leaders wicked; they called themselves wicked. They knew that Jesus was talking about them and they also knew that Jesus was the son of the landowner. That was how Jesus answered their question, *"By what authority are You doing these things? And who gave You this authority?" (Matthew 21:23 NKJV)*.

Third, we have the parable of the wedding feast, which we are studying in depth here.

c) Quick comparisons to help us better understand this parable

1. In the first two parables, God is _____ work from two sons and fruit from the vinedressers. But in this

unique third parable, God is not commanding anything. In fact, He has prepared everything and all the guests have to do is come, eat, and feast. The king's invitation to feast with him reminds us of God's command in the Old Testament that we love Him. But the New Testament tells us that God so loved the world, us.

2. In this parable, guests don't _____ to kill any animals, prepare anything, or even bring their own wedding garments. Everything will be provided for you.

3. Three times in Matthew, chapters 9, 22, and 25, we read about a wedding ceremony and a groom, but nothing is mentioned about the _____. That's because the earthly bride, Jerusalem, was not ready. And the heavenly bride, the church, was not born yet as Jesus had not yet been crucified.

d) Understanding the Three invitations.

1. **Come to the _____ (before the cross).** These announcements were provided by Old Testament servants because nothing was scheduled yet. The invitees simply didn't care.

> *"Or do you show contempt for the riches of his kindness, forbearance and patience, not realizing that God's kindness is intended to lead you to repentance?" (Romans 2:4 NKJV).*

2. **Come to the wedding everything is** _____
   (after the cross through the book of Acts). The invitees
   made light and many neglected the invitation. Neglecting
   God's invitation might be the most dangerous thing anyone
   can do. *"How shall we escape if we neglect so great a*
   salvation, which at the first began to be spoken by the Lord,
   and was confirmed to us by those who heard Him,"
   (Hebrews 2:3 NKJV). This invitation was by the New
   Testament disciples after the Lamb of God was slain and
   God had prepared everything. Jesus said on the cross, "It is
   finished."

   > *"Jesus said, 'Come to Me, all you who labor and*
   > *are heavy laden, and I will give you rest.'"*
   > *(Matthew 11:28 NKJV)*.

3. **Come to the wedding -** _____. This
   pertains to current times. The Lord is no longer looking for
   the worthy. He is looking for anyone who accepts the
   invitation. The great commission is to go to the whole
   world and spread the gospel. Today, people are coming
   from all over the world and becoming part of the bride, or
   the church. It doesn't matter your gender, marital status,
   color, race, educational level, or anything else. We find
   great examples of the church including many different
   people in the book of Acts. A respectable woman was
   saved, a woman with evil spirits was saved, a jail guard, as
   well as Saul (Paul) were saved.

All that matters is your answer to God's question, "Would you accept the invitation?" God will accept everyone, but not everyone will accept Him. All we have to do is come to Jesus and we will be saved.

> "Look to Me, and be saved, all you ends of the earth! For I am God, and there is no other. (Isaiah 45:22)

e) Three directions people in the parable went

1. **Some went to** _____ represents the cares of the flesh – Jesus warns against cares of the flesh on many occasions. Remember the sower parable in Matthew 13.

2. **Some went to** _____ represents the desires of the world – Jesus warns us about the cares of the world and the deceitfulness of riches that could lead to choking God's word. Nothing is wrong with business and money, as long as they don't provide an excuse to keep us away from God.

3. **Some** _____ **the servants** represents those killed for the Gospel. Why did they murder the servants? The servants announced that dinner was ready and extended the invitation. If those invited didn't want to go, they didn't have to kill the servants to make their point. The book of Acts is full of God's servants being murdered.

Even though they all went different ways, the honored guests all went the wrong way.

"All we like sheep have gone astray; We have turned, every one, to his own way; And the Lord has laid on Him the iniquity of us all" *(Isaiah 53:6 NKJV).*

The honored guests refused to attend the wedding because they were preoccupied with worldly things and not eternal life. Jesus wanted to make this point again; we should not be preoccupied with temporal things. Jews had no excuses because they had advance notice that the Messiah was coming. And finally, the Pharisees had even seen John the Baptist letting them know that "dinner was served" (the Messiah is here).

f) Three messengers –

1. **Servants** – The first servants represent the Old Testament _____ who came with the invitation to come back to the Lord. They refused the invitation from the servants.

2. **More servants** – The second servants to go out represent the New Testament _____ who offered an invitation to come back to the Lord. God's patience is immeasurable, and he sent more servants after He had done everything that needs to be done on the cross. And still, the ungrateful guests killed His message bearers. The king shows his patience once again in the parable by extending

the invitation again by sending additional servants, letting them know that dinner is ready.

3. **Armies** – A day will come when God _____ everyone, and the earth will be destroyed. His doors will be closed forever.

g) Wedding Garment

1. The king found a man not wearing the proper clothing for the wedding. The man was _____ because the garments for the wedding were provided.

2. God has provided proper robes. The _____ of salvation through Jesus Christ. If you want to meet the king, you must wear clothing appropriate to meet the king.

3. Good deeds are not good enough to be in the _____ of the Holy one. Our own attire, robes of righteousness, will never be enough. Only God's robes of righteousness will suffice.

4. When we live in _____, we don't see how bad our clothes are. But once we meet the Holy King face-to-face and His light shines, we will see how corrupt we are. When Isaiah, a prophet of God, saw the Lord, he discovered how sinful he was and shares the revelation in Isaiah 6.

5. The king didn't ask the underdressed guest why he was wearing the _____ clothes. Rather, he asked how the man got in. Had the man entered the right way

through the door, he would have been given the proper attire. Jesus is the door, and we must enter through Jesus.

h) For many are called, but few are chosen

1. Jesus is not saying that God _____ chose some people to go to Heaven while others go to hell. In fact, outer darkness and the weeping and gnashing of teeth is simply the regrets of those who are outside the hall of the wedding feast. They are not inside, with the food, the light, and the dancing, but in the darkness outside.

2. Jesus is making clear that the Jews are in fact God's chosen people, but if they don't live up to the reason why they were chosen by God, which is to live _____, God will simply choose others, such as prostitutes, thieves, and tax collectors.

3. Jesus is saying that while many people were called to _____ in His Kingdom, only those who show up are "chosen" to join in the festivities. Those who accept the invitation decide to be chosen.

4. But you have to come in the _____ way, which is through the front door, for only in this way will the guests be properly attired to live, serve, and function within God's Kingdom.

5. Finally, the servants went into the street and invited the bad and the good. Bad was mentioned before good as God has no _____ in those who respond to the call.

VI.   Conclusion

Come as you are. It doesn't matter if you are a sinner or killer, or feeling unworthy. He has new clothing for you. He will fix what's broken in your life. But don't delay because you never know if you will live another minute. Act now.

VII.   Homework

If you accepted the invitation, you are invited to go invite others. The simplest words can bring the biggest harvest. Go and tell others about Jesus; become a servant.

Notes:

_____

_____

_____

_____

Notes:

VIII.   Middle-Eastern Recipe

HUMMUS

INGREDIENTS

1½ cups canned chickpeas, reserve liquid
1 clove garlic, peeled and crushed
½ cup water, divided
4 tablespoons tahini
¼ cup liquid reserved from the canned chickpeas
1 tablespoon Lemon juice
pinch of salt
For garnish:
Chopped fresh parsley
½ tablespoon paprika
1 teaspoon sesame seeds
2 tablespoons olive oil
Serve with pita bread or grilled meat

METHOD

Using a food processor or blender, mix chickpeas with garlic and ¼ cup of water until smooth. Dissolve tahini in remaining ¼ cup water, ¼ cup reserved chickpea liquid and lemon juice, then blend with into chickpea mixture until smooth. Paste will be thick. Season with salt.

Pour hummus into dish and garnish with parsley, paprika, sesame seeds and/or olive oil. Serve with pita bread or grilled meats.

CHAPTER 5

The Rich Fool

Parables DECODED of Jesus

I. Bible Passage

a. Reading (Luke 12:16-21)

"¹⁶Then He spoke a parable to them, saying: "The ground of a certain rich man yielded plentifully. ¹⁷And he thought within himself, saying, 'What shall I do, since I have no room to store my crops?' ¹⁸So he said, 'I will do this: I will pull down my barns and build greater, and there I will store all my crops and my goods. ¹⁹And I will say to my soul, "Soul, you have many goods laid up for many years; take your ease; eat, drink, and be merry."' ²⁰But God said to him, 'Fool! This night your soul will be required of you; then whose will those things be which you have provided?' ²¹So is he who lays up treasure for himself, and is not rich toward God."

b.   **Explanation of the Parable**

A rich man's fields produced an excessive harvest beyond the capacity of his storage barns.. So he decided to knock down his existing barns and build bigger ones to keep all the crops. He saw he had plenty, he thought *I have plenty for crops that will last for many years. Take it easy. Eat, drink, and enjoy life.* Little did this man consider that he would die that night in view of his eternity. And Jesus advised His followers that this is exactly what's going to happen to those who store treasures for themselves on earth and are not generous toward God.

c. **Cultural Relevance**

Jesus had just finished dining with a group of Pharisees. After He left, many thousands gathered to listen to Him. Despite the enormous crowd waiting to hear Him speak, He began by addressing things only to His close group of disciples. His brief discourse expressed how valuable people were and how worthless possessions truly are, how they should fear God and not man, how they should protect and proclaim with confidence the Name of Christ, and that disowning the Holy Spirit leads to death.

Then, someone in the crowd called out to Jesus, "Teacher, tell my brother to divide the inheritance with me." Dividing inheritance was customary in that day and age. Although Jesus responded to this seeming interruption, He bypassed what the man specifically asked in order to get to the heart of the issue. Jesus used this particular question to address the attitude, not only of the man asking the question, but of the entire crowd. Desiring wealth is something everyone would identify with. With this in mind, He began His parable of the Rich Fool.

Jesus could have used a number of different illustrations, but He chose agriculture because the crowd would easily understand and readily identify with it. The Parable of the Rich Fool is one of Jesus' most direct parables. Those present did not have to try to figure out what was being communicated; it was quite clear.

II.   Occasion/Reason why Jesus Tells this Parable

Luke 12:13-14 tells us, "Then one from the crowd said to Him, 'Teacher, tell my brother to divide the inheritance with me.'" [14] But He said to him, "Man, who made Me a judge or an arbitrator over you?"

III.   Main lesson to Learn from the Parable
a. Be careful of _____ or covetousness.
b. _____ your treasures in Heaven. Your heart will always be where you are storing treasure. If your treasures are in Heaven, then you are doing things that please God. If your focus is on earth, then your efforts please your self.

c. More lessons can be taught if you will be _____ to the Holy Spirit.

d. The rich fool does not represent those who are wealthy. He represents individuals who attribute their wealth to their _____ and do not give God glory for blessing them in this way. All wealth, whether great or small, is a gift from God and is to be used to bring glory to Him and not to meet selfish desires.

e. The rich fool represents anyone whose life is marked by covetousness. This could easily be a poor person. The issue is not money in the bank, but the _____ of the heart.

f. Earthly _____ are not an indicator of spiritual health. Therefore, eternal riches and not temporal, earthly wealth, are to be sought.

"What good is it for a man to gain the whole world, and yet lose or forfeit his very self?" (Luke 9:25).

Some Points to consider:

- It's sad to see brothers fight. The brother who asked Jesus to divide the inheritance was in a dispute with family, but selfishness is recorded as early as the beginning of history with Cain and Able.

- Jesus was preaching a sermon scholars call "The Friend's Sermon". He preached to his disciples, even though an unnumbered multitude were gathered around him.

- A man apparently interrupted Jesus with a topic completely different from what Jesus was talking about, showing he was thinking about inheritance instead of Jesus' message. That's why Jesus continued his sermon after the parable. That man showed he was thinking about inheritance (something different).

- The man came to Jesus, but his heart was somewhere else. So many people go to church and their hearts are elsewhere.

IV.   Makeup of the parable

1. Ground   –   source   of _____ or business

2. Crops – income/_____

3. Rich   Man   –   one   who   cares   about _____ and themselves "ONLY"

4. Plentifully – _____

5. Soul – the _____ part between our body (flesh) and our spirit (which speaks to God)

6. Fool – those who don't _____ in God or forget God

V.   Discussion

a.   Closer Look at the Rich Man

<u>Good Qualities about the Rich Man:</u>

i.   He was a _____. (verse 17 "And he thought within himself.")

ii. He was a _____ man.

iii. He was one of _____. Because few are rich and many are poor.

iv. He was _____. His land was so fruitful that his old storage system wasn't big enough.

v.   He was a _____. In verse 18 we see, "So he said, 'I <u>will</u> do this...'". So he was active and willing to work. Also, he was working in the day and thinking at night.

vi. He was a _____. He had a step-by-step plan.

vii. He was _____. Most likely he was a young man because he said in verse 19: "Soul, you have many goods laid up for many years."

After all that, Jesus called him a "FOOL."

Notes:

_____

_____

So Why Was He a FOOL?

1. He was a fool because he did not _____ God. He used his own thoughts!

   "He who trusts in his own heart is a fool, But whoever walks wisely will be delivered." Proverbs 28:26

2. He thought _____ of himself and not of others. He had no room to store his crops. What about the houses of poor people or widows?

3. He _____ he would live for a long time. He didn't say, "If the Lord is willing and I live". He forgot that man's days are in God's hands.

4. He created earthly _____. Throughout scripture we are instructed about where we should store our treasures: In heaven. This man said, there I will store <u>all</u> my crops and my goods. They say, "don't put all your eggs in one basket", but this man did!

5. He calculated his days in "_____".

   "Do not boast about tomorrow, For you do not know what a day may bring forth... ." Proverb 27:1

6. He decided to feed the _____ the rest of his life, to live the rest of his life in ease. He planned to eat, drink, and be merry instead of to glorify God.

7. He thought he could find _____ in the world. But only one person can give rest, Jesus.

"Come to Me, all you who labor and are heavy laden, and I will give you rest." (Matthew 11:28)

8. He _____ I-itis.

"'What shall I do, since I have no room to store my crops?' ¹⁸So he said, 'I will do this: I will pull down my barns and build greater, and there I will store all my crops and my goods. ¹⁹And I will say to my soul... .'" (Luke 12:17-19).

His focus was on I, as was Satan in his original sin.

"How you have fallen from heaven, O star of the morning, son of the dawn! You have been cut down to the earth, You who have weakened the nations! "But you said in your heart, 'I will ascend to heaven; I will raise my throne above the stars of God, And I will sit on the mount of assembly In the recesses of the north. 'I will ascend above the heights of the clouds; I will make myself like the Most High'" (Isaiah 14:12-20 NKJV).

9. He told his soul to _____. What does the soul have to do with wealth?

Notes:

_____

_____

_____

_____

b. **Man and Covetousness** - Jesus was _____ us against covetousness, (desiring what belongs to others) because it causes division in business, churches, and even in families, especially when dividing inheritance. Covetousness is dangerous. Therefore the Bible compares it to:

• **Being Unclean**

"Who, being past feeling, have given themselves over to lewdness, to work all uncleanness with greediness" (Ephesians 4:19).

• **Accursed children**

"Having eyes full of adultery and that cannot cease from sin, enticing unstable souls. They have a heart trained in covetous practices, and are accursed children" (2 Peter 2:14).

• **Idolatry**

"Therefore put to death your members which are on the earth: fornication, uncleanness, passion, evil desire, and covetousness, which is idolatry" (Colossians 3:5).

c. **Man and God** – Jesus described a covetous man as a " _____ ". Who is the fool then?

   1. The Bible describes a person who doesn't believe in God as a FOOL. *"The fool has said in his heart, 'There is no God'" (Psalm 14:1).*

2. The rich man's discourse tells us that he forgot that God is the source of life and God is the one that gives life or takes it. The rich man forgot that God has full authority.

d. **Man and money** – wealth and money are _____ a sin and there is nothing inherently wrong with them.

"For the <u>love</u> of money (not money) is a root of all kinds of evil, for which some have strayed from the faith in their greediness" (1 Timothy 6:10 emphasis added).

e. **Man and his desire** – note that this rich fool only thought of _____. Note how many times he said "I" and "my".

Notes:

_____

_____

_____

_____

_____

_____

_____

VI.   Conclusion

a. If God _____ this type of man a "fool", we need to make sure not to do the same thing.

b. The Bible never mentions any _____ work that came from the rich fool. So God will not ONLY judge us on the evil we did, but also on the " _____ " that we did not do!

c. Remember that Jesus didn't come to judge (condemn) the world but to _____ the world.

d. Greed or covetousness was the _____ sin that caused Satan to fall. Also, the first sin Adam fell into, as he was greedy to eat from what didn't belong to him.

e. The wealthy fool was not ready to hear *"This night your soul will be required of you; then whose will those things be which you have provided?"* Be _____ anytime. Store your treasures in heaven. Some of the poorest people are richer than most wealthy people.

f. Wealth is temporary, but _____ is forever.

Notes:

_____

_____

How to Be Rich in God's Sight (practical tips)

1. Serve with joy! Every task you involve yourself in can be a blessing if done with joy.

2. Do everything with the knowledge that you are working for the Lord and not for man! Colossians 3:23-24 states, *"Whatever you do, work at it with all your heart, as an inheritance from the Lord as a reward. It is the Lord Christ you are serving."*

3. Invest in the lives of others! Look for ways to be a blessing in your church, to your family, your neighbors, and to those who are less fortunate than yourself.

4. See every trial as an opportunity from God to grow you and help you store up treasure in Heaven.

5. Fear God and not man. The introduction to this parable is a clear command, which all believers must heed with sober minds. *"I tell you, my friends, do not be afraid to show you whom you should fear: Fear him who, after the killing of the body, has power to throw you into hell. Yes, I tell you, fear him"* (Luke 12:4-5). In other words, we must always consider the fact that answering to God is of a far greater significance than having to answer to man. Again, the issue is temporal versus eternal.

VII. Homework

a. Moving forward, let us start doing two simple things all the time

    i. Consult the Lord (Make the Bible our roadmap for life.)

    ii. Seek the Lord (do His will first and put Him first)

Jesus warned His listeners. "Watch out! Be on your guard against all kinds of greed." Each person should consider, "What do I run after that will not last? What good thing am I neglecting because of my selfish pursuits?'"

_____

_____

_____

_____

_____

The purpose of life is not to eat, drink, and be merry! The purpose of life is summarized in the following two passages:

- Matthew 22:36-40 – *"Teacher, which is the greatest commandment in the Law?" Jesus replied: "'Love the Lord your God with all your heart and with all your soul and with all your mind.' The second is like it: 'Love your neighbor as yourself.' All the Law and the Prophets hang on these two commandments."*

- 1 Corinthians 10:31 – *"So whether you eat or drink or whatever you do, do it all for the glory of God."*

With the purpose of life in mind, how can you apply these scriptures to your life today in a new way?

_____

_____

_____

_____

_____

God has promised to take care of all our earthly needs, not all of our wants, but all our needs. In our culture we often confuse the two. See Matthew 6:25-34 to see God's promise of provision. What are some things you have considered needs that are actually wants? In what new ways can you trust God for your needs?

_____

_____

_____

_____

_____

_____

VIII.   Middle-Eastern Recipe

FOOL MEDAMMAS *(Simmered Fava Beans)*

Fool Medammas (or *Fool Mudammas*, *Ful Mudammas*, etc., often just called *Fool* or *Fuul*) is an Egyptian bean stew often eaten for breakfast sold by street vendors as Egyptian fast food. The basic recipe is *fool* (fava) beans, cooked until tender, mashed then mixed with olive oil and seasonings, typically lemon juice and cumin. The mashed beans are usually served garnished with egg and pita bread.

INGREDIENTS

    3 cups (about two pounds) dry small fava beans*
    ½ cup split red lentils, washed, rinsed, and cleaned
    1 ripe tomato, chopped
    1 onion, chopped (optional)
    4 cloves garlic, crushed (optional)
    1 tablespoons cumin
    1/4 cup lemon juice
    salt to taste
    1/4 cup olive oil

Optional Ingredients:
    ¼ cup finely chopped cucumber and tomato (optional)
    1 bunch green onions (scallions), chopped (optional)
   ground cayenne pepper or red pepper, to taste
   1 handful fresh parsley chopped
   one bunch green onions (scallions), chopped
   4 hard-boiled eggs

METHOD

- Wash and rinse fava beans and lentils with cold water. Drain before cooking.
- Add the fava beans and lentils to a slow cooker. Add tomatoes, onion and garlic if desired and cover the rest of the way with boiling water. Cook on high for 8-10 hours until the beans are tender, making sure the water is not completely evaporated. Add boiling water as needed.
- Mash beans with potato masher or fork. Stir in cucumbers, tomatoes and onions as desired, cumin, lemon juice, salt, and olive oil. Season with salt, and cayenne pepper to taste.
- Place serving-sized portions into bowls. Garnish with parsley, green onion, and sliced hard-boiled egg. Serve warm with warmed pita bread. (Can be stored in the refrigerator and re-heated or frozen prior to seasoning.)

Though not traditional, this dish could also be prepared with pinto beans (as used to make refried beans in Mexican cuisine); fool and pita bread is not that different from refried beans and tortillas.

* If you do not want to cook the beans yourself, you can buy canned beans at a Middle-Eastern market.

CHAPTER 6

The Pharisee and the Tax Collector

Parables
d≡C0Ɔ≡D
Of Jesus

I. Bible Passage

a. Reading Luke 18:10-14 NIV

"10Two men went up to the temple to pray, one a Pharisee and the other a tax collector. 11 The Pharisee stood and prayed thus with himself, 'God, I thank You that I am not like other men - extortionists, unjust, adulterers, or even as this tax collector. 12 I fast twice a week; I give tithes of all that I possess.' 13 And the tax collector, standing afar off, would not so much as raise his eyes to heaven, but beat his breast, saying, 'God, be merciful to me a sinner!' 14 I tell you, this man went down to his house justified rather than the other; for everyone who exalts himself will be humbled, and he who humbles himself will be exalted."

b. Explanation of the Parable

Two men went up to pray at the temple. A religious man, a Pharisee, and a tax collector went to pray at the temple. The Pharisees didn't like tax collectors.

The arrogant/pompous Pharisee went inside and reminded God in his prayer of all the good things he had done, while the tax collector stood far away from the temple and asked God for forgiveness. God heard and honored the prayer of the sinner rather than the religious man. Then Jesus went on to say that whoever exalts himself will be humbled (lowered). And whoever humbles (lowers) himself will be exalted.

c. Cultural relevance

Most tax collectors were Jews who worked for the Romans. Therefore, they were not respected by their own people. Tax collectors were considered reprehensible because they collected money from Jews and gave it to the Romans. They also had a reputation as dishonest, crooked men.

II.   Occasion/Reason why Jesus Tells this Parable

Jesus was addressing those who trusted in their own righteousness. Sad to say, this type of person still exists today.

"He spoke this parable to some who trusted in themselves that they were righteous, and despised others" (Luke 18:9)

III. **Main lesson of this Parable**

a.   Have a unpretentious _____ when praying.

b.   Repent - it's not by _____ that we are saved.

c.   Be humble for God to _____.

d.   Appearing to worship is not a _____ of a true worshiper.

IV. Composition of the Parable

a.   Temple – was a physical place of worship. But today, our _____ is the temple. Who is inside you? The Pharisee or the tax collector?

b.   Pharisee – _____ or self-righteous people

c.   Tax Collector – _____ or those who are far from God

V. Discussion

a) General Background about Pharisees

    i. Recognized as _____ men

    ii. _____ and respected by the Jews

    iii. Required to learn and memorize the _____ (Old Testament scriptures)

    iv. _____ the Torah

    v. Observed the law _____

b) General Background about Tax Collectors

    i. Worked for the _____, so they were considered "_____" by the Jews

    ii. _____ taxed people to build their own wealth (thieves)

    iii. Acted _____

    iv. _____ with murderers, adulterers, robbers, and other "sinners"

c) Closer Look at the Pharisee's Actions

1) Went to the temple not to _____ with God, but instead went to show-off his own good works.

2) Started by _____ God for how good he himself was.

3) Harbored religious _____ such as fasting, uttering long prayers, and giving to charity. These good works can make us feel that we are better than others.

4) Didn't _____ anything from God; he just spoke highly of himself.

5) Prayed _____ anyone else, and his prayer was long and eloquent.

6) Stood proudly in the temple instead of stand far away like the tax collector. He felt _____ to be in the temple.

d) Closer Look at the Tax Collector's Actions

1) _____ far away. He felt unworthy to be in the presence of God.

2) Wouldn't raise his eyes to Heaven. He knew Heaven was a _____ place and he was a sinner

3) _____ that he was a sinner.

4) Beat his chest – to show that he was _____ about his past

5) Spoke a _____ prayer asking for grace, called himself a sinner, and asked for mercy

The Pharisee and the Tax Collector Side-by-Side

Pharisee's actions/words	Tax Collector's actions/words
Went into the Temple	Went up to the Temple
Prayed to hear himself	Prayed to God
Felt worthy	Stood afar off
Appeared thankful that he was better off	Expressed gratefulness for grace of God
Announced proudly his great work	Couldn't raise his eyes to Heaven
Confessed no shortcoming or sin, but judged himself better than adulterers or even this tax collector	Confessed he was a sinner
Fasted twice a week	Had nothing to say about his good works
Gave 10% of ALL that he owned	Took from and stole from people
Enjoyed the respect of people	Incurred the hate of people
People looked up to him	People look down at him
Visited the temple to show-off	Visited the temple to seek God
Felt he was better than everyone	Felt he wasn't worthy
Prayed a long self-serving message with no appeal for grace	Prayed simply to thank God for grace and to be forgiven
Didn't ask God for anything	Asked God for forgiveness

VI. Conclusion

a. Salvation is only by _____ - not by works.

b. Mercy is _____ only on God's love - not by works.

c. Our works _____ are not enough, even if we go above and beyond .

    (i) The Pharisee fasted _____ a week, more than the law required.

    (ii) The religious man gave tithes of _____ that he possessed although the law required tithes only on certain items (See Deuteronomy 14:22-23).

God considers the heart behind our prayers. Confessing our sins is like music in God's ears more than any work or good deed we could ever do. God loves for us to honor Him, fast, and tithe, but He cares about the heart behind all the good work. It's ok to feel unworthy, because He will exalt us.

The parable of the Pharisee and tax-collector is a contrastive story with one basic message, summarized by Jesus' final statement: He who exalts himself will be humbled and he who humbles himself will be exalted. The Pharisee is an example of the first, and the tax-collector, the second. Therefore, the opposite attitude reflected our relationship with God in this life, will characterize our experience in the next.

Notes

VII. Homework

The Pharisee and the tax collector were figurative of typical attitudes that are common even in our age today. One man was full of pride and self-righteousness. The other was humble; he recognized his sins and asked for God's mercy and was justified.

Which do you identify more with? Why or why not?

_____

_____

_____

_____

_____

_____

Essentially, this parable is about the attitude of the heart. Having the right attitude is one of those things that you cannot afford to neglect as a follower of Christ.

Do you recognize any heart attitudes in your life that need adjusting?

_____

_____

_____

_____

Everybody faces difficult life circumstances although situations are different from one individual to another. Some might have a life more harsh than others. But challenges are not where the Bible puts the emphasis. From God's perspective, the events, as difficult as they may be, matter far less than the way we deal with them.

How do we react to the circumstances of life? What is our attitude when something happens to us? That's what matters to God. And this parable describes to us the attitude of the heart He commends. How does that apply to your life?

_____

_____

_____

_____

_____

From your heart, pray the prayer David prayed in Psalm 139:23-24, *"Search me, O God, and know my heart: try me, and know my thoughts. And see if there be any wicked way in me, and lead me in the way everlasting."*

VIII. Middle-Eastern Recipe

BASBOOSA
(Semolina Almond Coconut Cake)

Basboosa (or *Harrissa*) is a Middle-Eastern dense, sweet dessert. Often it is served with tea or Turkish coffee at the end of a meal.

Basboosa
> 2 cups ground medium semolina
> 1 cup sugar
> 2 tablespoons baking powder
> ½ cup shredded coconut
> 2 cups milk
> ⅔ cup unsalted butter (melted, clarified preferred)
> 2 cups sour cream or yogurt
> 2 teaspooons vanilla extract

Syrup
- 2 cups sugar
- 2 cups water
- 1 tablespoon lemon juice
- 2 teaspoon rose or orange blossom water (optional)

Garnish:
Approx. 20 whole almonds

METHOD

Preheat oven to 375 degrees F.

Begin with garnish

Boil almonds for 1 minute. Rinse with cold water. Slip skins off.

Cake

Combine all the ingredients for the basboosa and mix well.

Transfer the batter to a 9 x 13 buttered baking pan. Score basboosa lightly into desired shapes, traditionally squares or diamonds. Place blanched almonds on top of each shape.

Bake for 40 minutes until lightly golden brown. Basboosa is ready when a toothpick comes out clean.

Pour syrup below on top of hot basboosa.

Cut along score lines and let basboosa cool completely before serving.

Syrup

Combine sugar, water and lemon juice. Boil for 10 minutes.

Add rose or orange blossom water and stir well.

CONCLUSION

Parables **decoded** of Jesus

As we reflect upon our journey together through these five parables, let us take a bird's-eye view of what common thread we can find. While we can draw many similarities, we want to elaborate upon that fact that all of these parables appear to provide a simple story. But upon further examination, we see a deeper common truth.

In the parable of the sower, we see different types of grounds. At first glance, the seeds that fell on similar ground appear similar. So too in our relationships. We can quickly judge another based on our experiences and pay close attention to the type of "ground" their heart is, thus passing up an opportunity for right ministry or friendship. If I see another as good ground at first contact and don't seek to understand that they actually have hard, compacted, hurt ground, I can easily dismiss them as being someone who just doesn't like me, easily taking offense. This can be applied to each type of ground, and my response determines how I can plant seeds in others' lives that will grow to bear fruit if I correctly examine grounds that need cultivation.

In the parable of the ten virgins, appearances play a major

role again. All ten girls look similar, and a reader can be easily deceived into thinking this parable is unfair. However, if we choose to lean into what God is saying and understand that our outward holiness and our own good works can never get us into Heaven, then we can understand how to better love and relate to the five virgins who ran out of oil. We should seek to bring truth, clarity and understanding to an otherwise religious appearing individual.

In the parable of the wedding feast, once again we are tempted to pass judgment upon God as being a harsh king for the act of throwing out a guest who came to the marriage feast in his own clothes. But when we fully realize that our own righteousness can never measure up to the righteous robes God has provided us as a gift, then we can respond with gratefulness and not by trying to earn anything that we could never pay for anyway. Appearances also play an important role in this parable in that those who appeared qualified and were the first to be invited rejected the invitation. Sometimes those we assume have life all figured out are the ones with the highest walls separating them from God.

In the parable of the foolish rich man, appearances again play a role. A man who at first glance looks like he has it all together, but Jesus showed deeper insight. God cautioned us about leaving Him out of the equation and relying solely on our own abilities. The rich foolish man felt that he had no room in his life for God and that his wealth and good fortune were his doing alone.

Then God stepped in and let him know otherwise. May our dependence be on God first and foremost, allowing Him to lead us in His way, and may we not appear wise in our own eyes.

And finally in the parable of the Pharisee and tax collector we see a comparison of two men. One is highly esteemed, appearing righteous in his own eyes and in the eyes of his community. The other knew how low he had fallen and was in need of salvation. Be careful to discern first within ourselves whether we have a Pharisee attitude. Also consider others who appear to have it all together. No one is too high and righteous to fall from pride. It is a very slippery slope because it is a condition of the heart that creeps in and takes over. God helps us to remain humble when we choose to stay close to the Source.

God is perhaps asking us not to be quick critics of appearances and pass verdicts on others in a moment of judgment. Making snap decisions based on a person's looks, dress, or even denomination hinders the door of open communication if we have a preconceived notion that clouds our thoughts about them.

For further study

After studying the parables, we must

- Live every lesson behind the parables here on earth.
- Use what we learned for God to give us personal devotions from Bible readings.

- Take a parable and choose one word, such as oil, and expand the study of that word from the Scriptures. Meditate on what we learn and see where God leads us. Keeping a journal of our studies and the changes we notice strengthens our faith.

- Examine ourselves daily with the measure of the Word of God. Many of us are just as guilty, and notice when we examine ourselves in comparison to others. But Jesus wants us to start examining ourselves against His Word. If I compare myself to a drug lord or a mass murderer, I might get the impression that I'm perfect. But the Bible is the true measure of my thoughts, acts and deeds. Therefore, daily, we need to look at ourselves in the mirror and ask if we are pretending to be who we are? If my life were on a big screen 24/7 in front of other people who could see every thought and action, would I do the same things I'm doing now? Many of us examine ourselves against bad patterns, and we judge ourselves much better than "them", but Jesus wants us to examine our good habits, as they might look good but are actually corrupt.

Notes:

Notes:

Notes:

ANSWERS

ANSWER KEY:

Introduction to the Parables:

Key Elements of the Parables

1. preached
2. 43-58
3. one-third
4. preserved
5. practical
6. response
7. Parables can be categorized in three sections:
   a. God, you
   b. believers
   c. non

4 Questions that Frequently Arise about the Parables:
1. mean
2. parables
3. speak
4. interpret

Q1. What does "parable" mean?

1. place   cast
2. like   looks
3. proverb

Definition of Parable:
illustrative
comparison

Q2. What are the parables?

Parables are:

1. nature life
2. simple brief
3. history culture
4. Earthly Heavenly
5. secrets
6. education
7. clarify
8. multitudes

Q3. Why did Christ speak in parables?

1. hunger
2. dull hear
3. special
4. separate

Q4. How do we interpret the parables?

1. Analyze
2. interpretation
3. assume
4. cultural historical
5. overanalyze
6. arrange
7. glean
8. understand
9. solely

Chapter 2: Parable of the Sower

a. Explanation of the Parable
<u>three</u>
<u>seeds</u>
<u>soil</u>

b. Cultural Relevance
1. When was this message preached?
   a. <u>already</u>
2. To whom was it preached?
   a. <u>multitude</u>
3. Where was it preached and why?
   a. <u>seaside</u>.
   b. <u>Roman</u>
   c. <u>boat</u>
4. What is a seed?
   <u>dry</u> and <u>dead</u>

3. Main lessons (thoughts) from the parable
   a. <u>hearts</u>
   b. <u>enemy</u>
   c. <u>teach</u>
   d. <u>always</u>

4. Composition of the sower parable

The Sower Parable is made up of three important elements:
The <u>Sower</u> - the <u>Seeds</u> - and the <u>Soil</u>

1. <u>Jesus,</u>   <u>Heaven</u>
2. <u>Word</u>
3. <u>people</u>

5. Discussion:
    1. Wayside (hard ground): <u>hear</u>
        <u>hearts</u> and <u>minds</u>
In the wayside soil, the enemy is <u>Satan</u>.

    2. Stony places (shallow ground):
        <u>fired</u> <u>depth</u>   <u>flesh</u>

    3. Thorns (distracted hearts):
        <u>busy</u> <u>leave</u>   <u>mad</u>

        c. The enemy is the <u>world</u>.

    4. Good Ground: <u>live</u>

6. Conclusion

Unclean Trinity

<u>world</u>   <u>devil</u>   <u>flesh</u>

<u>CHAPTER 3</u>: The Ten Virgins

c. Cultural Relevance
    1. <u>binding</u>
        a. <u>legally</u>
        b. <u>first</u>
        c. <u>after</u>
        d. <u>divorce</u>
        e. <u>control</u>

f. negotiated
g. Dowry
h. live
i. adultery

2. **ceremony**
    a. requirements
    b. ten
    c. house
    d. royalty

IV. **Main Lesson of this Parable**
    a. waiting   ready
    b. handed
    c. accepting
    d. wisdom and foolishness
    e. same

1. **Composition of the Parable**
    a. invited
    b. word
    c. Holy
    d. lack
    e. connection
    f. order
    g. Christ
    h. Feast
    i. Starts

V. **Discussion**

1. hour
2. outside
3. same   same

4. <u>law</u>   <u>grace</u>
5. <u>church</u>   <u>body</u>
6. <u>classification</u>
7. <u>energies</u>
8. <u>nature</u>
9. <u>coming</u>

Explanation of the "Foolish"

1. <u>denies</u>
2. <u>relies</u>
3. <u>doesn't</u>
4. <u>curses</u>
5. <u>light</u>
6. <u>quick</u>
7. <u>perverse</u>
8. <u>cross</u>

Explanation of the "Wise"

<u>opposite</u>

1. <u>lift</u>
2. <u>benefit</u>

Explanation of the "Bridegroom"

<u>pay</u>   <u>belonging</u>

Explanation of the "Oil"

<u>sign</u>

CHAPTER 4: Parable of the Wedding Feast

III. Main Lesson of the Parable

  a. response
  b. grace
  c. accept
  d. invitation
  e. excuses
  f. closes
  g. offers
  h. gracious

c) Quick comparisons to help us better understand this parable
1. commanding
2. need
3. Bride

d) Understanding the Three Invitations.
1. wedding
2. ready
3. anyone

e) Three directions people in the parable went
1. farm
2. business
3. murdered

f) Three messengers –
1. prophets
2. apostles
3. judges

g) Wedding Garment

1. speechless
2. garments
3. presence

4. <u>darkness</u>
5. <u>wrong</u>

h) For many are called, but few are chosen

1. <u>sovereignly</u>
2. <u>righteously</u>
3. <u>participate</u>
4. <u>right</u>
5. <u>preference</u>

CHAPTER 5: PARABLE OF THE RICH FOOL

III. Main lesson to Learn from the Parable

      a. <u>greed</u>

      b. <u>Store</u>

      c. <u>sensitive</u>

      d. <u>own abilities</u>

      e. <u>desire</u>

      f. <u>possessions</u>

IV. Makeup of the parable

1. <u>income</u>
2. <u>paycheck</u>
3. <u>money</u>
4. <u>successful</u>
5. <u>connecting</u>
6. <u>believe</u>

V.　Discussion
a.　Closer Look at the Rich Man

<u>Good Qualities about the Rich Man</u>

i. <u>thinker</u>

ii. <u>rich</u>

iii. <u>few</u>

iv. <u>fortunate</u>

v. <u>hard worker</u>

vi. <u>smart man</u>

vii. <u>young</u>

<u>So Why Was He a FOOL?</u>

1. <u>consult</u>
2. <u>ONLY</u>
3. <u>assumed</u>
4. <u>treasure</u>
5. <u>years</u>
6. <u>flesh</u>
7. <u>rest</u>
8. <u>had</u>
9. <u>rest</u>

b. Man and Covetousness - <u>warning</u>

c. Man and God – "<u>FOOL</u>"

d. Man and money – <u>not</u>

e. **Man and his desire** – <u>himself</u>

VI. Conclusion

        a. <u>labels</u>

        b. <u>evil</u>   "<u>good</u>"

        c. <u>save</u>

        d. <u>first</u>

        e. <u>ready</u>

        f. <u>eternity</u>

CHAPTER 6 – PHARISEE AND THE TAX COLLECTOR

III. Main lesson of this Parable

a. <u>spirit</u>

b. <u>works</u>

c. <u>hear you.</u>

d. <u>sign</u>

IV. Composition of the Parable

a. <u>body</u>

b. <u>Religious</u>

c. <u>Sinners</u>

V. Discussion

a. General background about Pharisees

i. religious

ii. Trusted

iii. Torah

iv. Taught

v. strictly

b. General Background about Tax Collectors

i. Romans   "traitors"

ii. Over

iii. dishonestly

iv. Classified

c. Closer Look at the Pharisee's Actions

1. talk

2. thanking

3. pride

4. need

5. before

6. worthy

d. Closer Look at the Tax Collector's Actions

2. Stood

3. holy

4. Confessed

5. <u>upset</u>

6. <u>brief</u>

VI. Conclusion

a. <u>grace</u>

b. <u>based</u>

c. <u>alone</u>
   i. <u>twice</u>
   ii. <u>all</u>

ABOUT THE AUTHORS:

HANY & DIANA ASAAD have a Middle Eastern upbringing and understand the culture distinctly with degrees in Biblical Studies. They have been in Christian ministry (primarily Arabic) for more than twenty years and are excited to bring this knowledge to a new audience in a relevant and original way. They are frequent guests on international television programs and satellite TV channels associated with *The 700 Club, Joyce Meyer Ministries* and *TBN*. They currently reside in the South with their three beautiful daughters.

Learn More at:
www.RelentlessLiving.com
www.HanyAsaad.com
www.DianaAsaad.com

Also Available:

www.ingramcontent.com/pod-product-compliance
Lightning Source LLC
Chambersburg PA
CBHW071558040426
42452CB00008B/1215